The Illusion of Freedom

Mike Gagnon

Published by Mike Gagnon, 2017.

While every precaution has been taken in the preparation of this book, the publisher assumes no responsibility for errors or omissions, or for damages resulting from the use of the information contained herein.

THE ILLUSION OF FREEDOM

First edition. October 27, 2017.

Copyright © 2017 Mike Gagnon.

ISBN: 978-1988369648

Written by Mike Gagnon.

Dedicated to our unborn descendants, that they may be truly free.

Introduction

This is the beginning of a recording that I never thought I would make, so follow with me as I get through it with as few distractions as possible.

First of all, I'm not going to say things like "this is going to blow your mind" or any other cliched fucking saying, because it's cliched and because I'm not going to use any fucking quips or embellishments or flourishes to try and make me sound fucking smarter than I am or to make me sound important and smarter than you. I'm not. So understand please that all the information included here is not me telling you, "oh I'm a fucking genius so I figured this out."

The crux of this message is that if you hear this or you read it I ask only I ask only that you be honest with yourself.

Talk to yourself and tell yourself how you really feel about everything, not just the words that you're listening to or reading, but ask yourself "why am I doing the things that I am doing in my life?".

Why are you worried about the opinions of people that you either don't know, or never see. When it really comes down to that, look at the world we live in. Look at the real world without any moral brainwashing one way or the other, to try and "turn a frown upside down" or "put on a happy face". Really just look at the world, look at the society we live in. Do you think it's OK? Do you agree with it? Honestly, can you look at the world we live in and not say that there's something wrong? There's something wrong, even if you can't put your finger on it even if you don't know what it is and how to verbalize it.

We compromise ourselves so much. We compromise ourselves mostly for money or for excuses that we use to justify our mission for money.

Think about it. Why do you have to give up your morals and ethics? Why do you have to compromise yourself? Why do you have to make yourself a slave to the person paying your wage? Even if you hate your job just to help and take care of your family? Aren't we supposed to be smarter than that? Aren't we supposed to be the smartest animals on Earth? We've been around for, you know, thousands and thousands of years, hundreds of thousands of years and we haven't figured out a better system yet? we haven't figured out how to take care of ourselves, without working jobs we hate and feeling like willing slaves? If anything we've moved in the opposite direction.

We've moved in the opposite direction. When I see that I mean: shouldn't we have figured out how to take care of ourselves and our families and loved ones by now with having to make ourselves a wage slave?

Shouldn't we have figured out how to be self-reliant and be in business to work together?

The society we live in, if anything is pulling us further apart. Wouldn't the fact that we're supposed to be programmed for survival mean that we would have figured out that the more we work together the larger our team of allies are, the better for everyone?

The Ravings of a Madman

There's something wrong here and there's something that's pulling us away from the natural order of things. Something has been changed. Something has been compromised and it's been compromised from the beginning. From the get go. I was very, very hesitant to start recording. I almost didn't. There's probably a number times that I should have recorded it before and I'm just finally doing it now. I was hesitant for so long because I was worried that I would be perceived as a madman, and that these would be the ramblings of a madman.

So the ravings of a lunatic. Except, I'm following my own advice.

I am doing what feels true and right and valid. Valid. These feelings are valid.

We should be better than this. I believe we are better than this and the systematic destruction of that certainty among the population screams of manipulation. We've been led astray somewhere, but I'm going to go back to that shortly.

First, I want to finish the point of not being a raving madman.

I don't believe I am a madman. I am perfectly sound in mind. Maybe not body, but that's a different issue. A little levity, that's all. Not breaking the rule of the stroke my own ego, which is what I was going to get back to as well.

So yes I understand even now, I'm rambling and will be very easy to take this as the ramblings of a madman. I'm going to build a case. I promise if you stay with this, if you keep listening, if you keep reading, I will make a case for this so compelling it may change your entire outlook on life. I'm not going to make you wait for some weird thing at the end or sell you something. You're skeptical probably right now rolling your eyes thinking, "Yeah I've read this before. This is just MLM sales copy.". You know, charlatan type stuff. Well, all I can say is if you're reading or listening to this, it cost you very little or nothing, because my intention from the start of this is to make this information as cheap and freely available as possible, so that the most number of people read it. I'm doing that because we need to be on the same side as human beings. We need to be on the same side, and in saying, I don't think I'm a madman.

Maybe the fact that I don't think I'm a madman is a sign that I'm a madman.

I don't know, but this is the first step in building some true honesty between you and I.

It's OK if you think I'm a madman.

It's OK if you read this and think I'm a raving lunatic or a con artist trying to get something from you or dupe impressionable people. You should think that way. You should, because we should be concerned about people taking advantage of the welfare and well-being of others. Not only that, but I am not going to spend an ounce of energy trying to convince you that I'm not a madman, because that's not what's important. My personal image isn't important, and you don't have to believe me. You could stop reading now and I wouldn't blame you. You could stop listening now, and that would be OK. Even if you never finished listening or reading, that's OK. I understand and I accept that you may go on with the rest of your life thinking I'm a lunatic and a charlatan.

What's important is that I tried. I tried to do what I thought was right. I tried to do what I thought would help anyone and everyone who reads or hears this, and I know I won't get everyone. I know that.

We live in a world where we have been taught to be skeptical. We've been taught to be distrustful of each other and that's the point.

Why?

Why is that so propagated and encouraged in our society? We've been around for so long. I know it's a blip. A blink of an eye in the history of the universe and the planet, but we're smart enough. We've been around long enough to figure out that the way our world works and the systems that we live under are not practical or beneficial to the largest number of people. Not to the regular citizens, only the very few in charge and those in charge politically are influenced by money from large businesses. For example, it's quite obviously a conflict of ethics and morals to have a politician elected to lead people and look out for their best interest, after having their election campaign funded by a business that profits from selling to those people. It's a clear cut case of conflict of interests and the only reason you might disagree, the only reason you might see it another way is because you have been conditioned and trained to believe that it's OK, but it's not.

How would we ever expect a president, a governor, a prime minister, an elected official, to ever be looking out for the interests of those who elected them in, when we allow large companies who want to sell us products or profit off of our labour or misfortune to fund the people that we would elect in? The people giving them the money that they are forced and required to have in order to even attempt to be elected and compete. Are we not already veering so far off of the original idea of democratic elections that alarm bells should be going off? If not, then there's a problem and it's not with us. It's with a system that has been set up to mislead us from the day that we're born.

When was the last time you honestly felt that your elected officials and politicians were really looking out for your best interest? How is it, around the world that governing bodies pass laws that are not popular with their populace? How do they pass laws that the majority do not agree with, and that people are worried about? How does that happen if elected officials making and passing those laws are representing those who voted them in? How do laws that are unpopular with the general public, ever get voted in or made? Why aren't we more informed about that?

They want us to not care and not be informed and not pay attention because they're looking out for themselves and their own interests. No politician in our current system is getting elected into office without tons of money. That money is coming from companies like Bayer and Coca-Cola and William Morris and Camel cigarettes and a million other places that represent conflicts of interests. How can we expect our elected officials to truly be concerned about the well-being of their own citizens that elect them in, when they are so indebted to those companies that profit from us doing things that are detrimental to our own well-being? McDonald's knows that their food is unhealthy and not recommended to be eaten on the frequency that most people do. Cigarette companies know their product kills. Know it. They know they know it, and they deny it because it's bad for business, not because it's bad for people. They want you to think that they represent freedom of choice and independence and not that they have you addicted to a drug, of which they are the dealer.

I don't know if that totally made sense, but they don't care. they don't care because, to them, money and power are more important than the well-being of a stranger. That is a fundamental flaw that should not exist in an evolved, intelligent race of human beings, of any race capable of cognitive thought. If we'd been left to our own devices, I'm confident we would have figured out the best way to work and live together in peace by now, but we haven't.

So what could have caused that? My feeling is it's manipulation from people who have found a way to profit from us not doing what we know is right and what we feel is true. By corrupting our judgment in ways that make them rich so they don't have to work or do anything.

This world, this planet, regardless of where it came from, whether you believe in a purely scientific explanation or a purely religious explanation, set aside the source. This planet we've been given as a gift, in one way or another, could be a paradise on earth while we are alive.

It could be in Eden and it's not because we're not working together and we have to have been able to figure that out by now.

We base our lives on a society that works around going and doing things we don't want to do in exchange for money to buy things that we don't need and it's just not logical.

This planet provides everything we need in this world. If we were able and willing to work together to help our neighbours, the whole idea of survival, how we even stay on this planet means that at one time we had to survive for ourselves. We didn't have easily accessible food. We didn't have shelter. We didn't have cities. We didn't have houses. Everyone had to know how to survive how, to live. Everyone had to be self-reliant, self-sufficient, independent but also help others. We didn't need to go and do some pointless job to make someone else rich so that they wouldn't have to do any work, in order to get money and monetary gain in order to care for our families at home, because we could care for our families at home without the money. At one time we could care for ourselves and our loved ones on our own, because we knew how to do it and we didn't need that money that we're trading our freedom for now.

And I do mean freedom. We're living in a dystopia. I will give you a heads up now. I had to get high to start saying this. So eventually, inevitably, someone is going to say these are the marijuana fuelled ravings of a madman. I mentioned before that it's just the crazy rambling of someone who's stoned off their tree. I'm not very high now. I have a slight buzz, but I had to get high in order to overcome my apprehension of just doing this.

I'm saying this, why? Why should I have such apprehension about talking to an inanimate machine that records my voice with a file I never have to share with anyone?

Marijuana

Why do I have to be afraid? Why, in the back of my mind am I so worried about how it's perceived? Why am I afraid to even record it, unless we're living in a dystopia and we're all in denial about it? Maybe we don't even realize it. I am pro-marijuana, and I think it helps. I think that's why it's been so vilified and restricted, because it truly does help the mind function better. Scientific testing has shown that the electrons in the brain continue to fire instead of firing and resting between pulses every few microseconds. Marijuana is what causes that electrical impulse to continue instead of taking breaks. That's why your thoughts are so much more intense and why you zero in on really deep concepts and ideas or you think your ideas are more significant when you're high and so forth. So I have realized it presents a case to disregard what I'm saying.

The fact that I have presence of mind to know that, I think, is a sign that perhaps some of those effects have been exaggerated in order to cause doubt in those who really say what is true and what they feel when they're high on marijuana.

I am pro marijuana I think it is a great thing. It has a lot of great uses. So I'll have to apologize, I'm getting high around doing this. Indulging in my munchies. If you're hearing this on the recording, this is part of my philosophy; not being perfect. This is because the only way you should be able to trust me, is that I'm not trying to convince you. Anyone trying to convince you of something too hard, trying to get you to come over to their way of thinking should not be trusted. They have to have ulterior motives that they want to use you as a pawn to achieve.

Historically, and smart people have noticed in their life, 99 percent of the time people using high pressure are not looking out for your best interests. They're looking for a way to profit from your insecurities and poor decisions. I don't want to do that. I don't want to instill any self doubt in your mind.

You have access to this information obviously, because you're listening and reading right now. Keep it and share it with people and if at any point in the future you want to come back and read the rest or listen to the rest, than do so. Whether it takes you five minutes or 50 years to revisit and consider the information I'm presenting, that's fine. Everyone has to come to their own realizations in their own way, in their own time. So where do I go from here. I don't feel like I've explained it much yet.

We're 20 minutes in (the recording) and I'm not even at the tip of the iceberg and going out to get a bit more high.

All right I'm working on it. I have to keep this right now because the thoughts are coming faster than my ability to keep thinking of really good examples.

I think even when I'm not recording I'm just going to keep getting high and keep talking. and hopefully this thing comes together.

Anyway, here's some theoretical evidence to prove my point.

What's in our food?

Let's look at food. The food industry. All these processed foods and ingredients, things that we've identified are problems, like high fructose corn syrup or just sugar in general. We know it's bad for us. We know that and then we live in this guilt. We turn it into a guilty pleasure. How self-destructive is that? Why is that encouraged? Why would we ever have started to use synthetic, fake, artificial things in our food? I'm not talking about colouring or things that are reasonably food safe. But do we really even know what that definition is? Because I'm not sure I do. But one thing I do know is that if something is completely fake, synthesized, made from questionable sources, why did we ever start putting that in food? To save money? Why would we let a company get away with putting things we know are bad for us and poisonous in our food? Why would we let them do that? Because we let them get started and we let them become too powerful before we ever knew how dangerous it was.

That's the only answer. It went back to the beginning of business. They started putting politicians in their pocket. Then the problem is, we're not going to fight with this company because they're the ones who poses the money that we need so that we can get the positions of power. Because we're greedy. I believe the best ruler, the best elected official would be someone who never wanted the job, instead of those that go after it. Those that go after it, at least in modern times, maybe it was more altruistic at one time, but in modern times they go after it for themselves. For power, for fame, for money, but not to help their fellow man. Not to help anyone else. Not to make life better. We could all be free. I'm really talking about freedom, real freedom, not this fake freedom we have.

We value freedom so much and we compromise it so much and we're giving back more of it and more of it every day, to try and feel safe. Safe from the people who caused the situations that create the feeling of unsafeness and insecurity.

I'm tired I'm going to try and keep going.

But know if I wake up I will continue when I wake up.

I haven't even started to prove these points, but let me tell you this: This is meant for you. This is meant for you to think about. These points are for every human being to consider and I do mean it. I may be known for writing fiction, but this isn't fiction. This is coming from the heart and I'm talking directly to you, not just the reader, but the person transcribing this. Yes, you. I may not know who you are, but there's a reason why I'm recording this and having it transcribed. It's to help spread the message. Help spread the information.

I want you to know and be aware of this and you can judge it on your own. You can embrace it, you can believe it and you can share it with others, or you can discard it. Every single person is worth the attempt. It is worth the try and every single person who hears these things and maybe thinks the same way I do, that's one more person that's going to help spread the message and spread the word. That's what we need, because what we need are things that bring us together not separate us, the way that our systems have been doing. We need to come together. Not a person. We don't need a hero, we don't need someone else to be elected to save us and represent us. That's how they got a hold before. That system has already been corrupted. We need to stand together as one united humanity and stop letting them divide us by age, race, gender and religion. Maybe all the religions are right or maybe none of them, or maybe one out of all of them is, but if your neighbour believes in a different religion, how does that affect you? Why would you feel the need to fight them, instead of accepting that they believe something else? If you truly, truly believe in your set of beliefs? If you truly think they're true and they're real, you should have the confidence to allow someone else their own journey. If you're confident that these are true and that they're obvious and that the proof is surrounding you, then why wouldn't

THE ILLUSION OF FREEDOM

you be confident that someone with a different set of beliefs would come around to yours, just by living? Just by experience in the world?

That's just one example.

Yes I'm talking to you. No matter what your race, your age, your colour, your beliefs. I want to help you. I want us to help each other. I want us to both be free and happy. That's what you should want for all of your fellow man; to be free and happy. To be able to live and love and be with the people that they can't live without. To take care of their families and to not suffer. We shouldn't just resign and say "the world doesn't work that way.". That's brainwashing. That's convincing us before we rise up. It's squashing a rebellion before it starts. We need people willing to start more than ever now. Translator, I'm talking to you too. Yes. You, the person listening. The person converting these words into type in English or French or Russian or anything.

You are important. We're all important. I'm not a leader. I'm just sharing the information. I don't want to lead the world. I want the world to come together because I think that's the only way we're going to survive. The people who corrupt the system and have taken control of it, are enjoying luxury on our suffering. We've allowed it to happen, because they've tricked us into complacency. This is a lesson that the human race had to have known, had to have learned at some point or would have if there hadn't been some sort of diabolical interference. How did someone at some unknown point in the past know that they could capitalize on misleading the human race, in every possible way. It's a good question and there could be a lot of theories. There could be a lot of theories and they could all be right and they could all be wrong. I'm not going to get into theories yet.

I will, and I things are going to keep getting heavier, but just think. Just look inside yourself.

Do you honestly agree with the world that we live in? The way things work? The policies that we live under?

Why aren't we helping each other more? Why are we more afraid of our neighbours, than friendly with them?

I had go to sleep last night, I was very tired, I don't know if you could tell. I'm awake again now and in the sober light of day I'm still coherent enough to continue with this train of thought because I truly believe in it. Further evidence that it's not just ramblings of someone who is high off their ass.

I know I'm jumping around from point to point here, but bear with me. I'm just saying my thoughts as they come in the stream of consciousness.

The separation of corporation and state

We worry about the separation of church and state. It's been a standard for a long time. People get upset and speak out against it when they feel that there's a clear conflict that church is interfering with state policy. That may very well be a good idea, but I believe that it's used as a distraction method. So we don't think about a more pressing issue. That is, that there should be a separation between business and state and that there's a much clearer conflict of interests at work against the public interest in the name of business and state in collusion together.

That is equally as compromising, if not more compromising, than church and state.

If religion and government should be separated, why should we not have business and corporate interests separate from politics? When you look at the philosophies of marketing, branding and advertising, those businesses are trying to get you to create a false emotional bond with them. They're trying to become the same kind of thing that religion is. We have faith in brands the way people used to have faith in their religion. I'm not saying that philosophy is a right or wrong, in a place of religion, but in the case of business, it's an inanimate figure, not even an object. It's a corporation, it's not even an ideal, but a man-made symbol with no more special attribute that any other figure man could scribble on a cave wall or chalkboard. It's that's never going to return or fulfill those imaginary things we want or those needs.

Anyone, anyone trying to convince you of their way of thinking is working against your best interests.

Anyone trying to change your feelings and opinions over to their side has ulterior motives. They have figured out how to profit off of a changing opinion in some way or benefit themselves.

In a world where everyone is truly doing what they feel is right, as long as they aren't harming anyone else, we should all be confident that everything is OK. We should be confident that what we are doing or feeling is just, but the entire system has been arranged to cause self-doubt. To question our own morality and ethics. To question our own sanity. To wonder if we're wrong and there's nothing wrong with that. Self-reflection is good. I'm not preaching that you should assume that every thought you have in your mind is right. When a religious or political leader tries to push you to hate or fear another person or group or culture, that's not really the kind of patriotism that it's passed off to be. It's purposely done to create a separation between you and them. Because if we were on the same side, if humanity was on the same side, the people in charge that oppress us, the people that oppress those in third world countries and second world countries and first world countries they wouldn't be able to maintain control and that's what it's about.

They're creating a paradise on Earth just for them, on your back and your sweat because they don't like to share. If we all work together, we could all be enjoying paradise on earth.

The world will provide all the food, water, shelter building materials, anything we need.

If you develop basic skills in producing livestock, produce, those sorts of things. If there's something that you don't have access to and can't do yourself, you should be able to find a neighbour or another person who can provide that in exchange your skills and talents. Better yet, your neighbour could teach you how to do it, wherever possible.

We've been brainwashed to think of things as goods and services.

Offer your skills and talents and exchange them for the things that you need, but only when you're not able to do it yourself. I'm not saying do it all yourself. Help your neighbour. Help your neighbour build his house or build his barn. Hell if we all just help each other more and gave each other things in appreciation. If a man comes and helps you build a pig pen or a barn or your house, give him one of your pigs in appreciation.

That's just an example. That way, he can eat because you appreciate his help and the way he helped you. You appreciate that he took his time and used his skills and abilities to help you as a decent human being, as a neighbour who is on the same side as you, regardless of his religious or political beliefs. Humanity needs to recreate a connection between the common man and not allow those in charge currently to pervert your perspective.

I know this sounds crazy, but it's true. It's true and it's honest and at some point in history somebody has had the insight enough to know that they could manipulate mankind that they could create a utopia for themselves on the backs of the poor.

And it's been going on for centuries maybe, decades at least. I feel definitely in the last century, the idea of humanity has become so perverted that it's harder to convince people that we should ignore our differences and work together than it is to work them up into an unreasonable hate of each other and distrust. That's what those in charge want. They keep dividing us. We have to give up the old biases. All these ideas that they have manipulated and implanted into us through whatever means is at their disposal. They've perverted the idea of science. They perverted the idea of honesty, of humanity, in order to manipulate us, so that they can provide for themselves on the suffering of everyone else.

It's like we're in 1984. I mean we're not that far off. We like to think we are, but if you read the book, look at the way people respond to things on the news. Celebrities are political figures. It's like our five minutes of hate. The five minutes hate where we are encouraged and brainwashed into hating a particular figure that represents something that isn't the same as our beliefs or our behaviours. And we're encouraged to hate and do horrible things and say horrible things. Why?

Why would a media system want to encourage that, unless it is run by those who profit from dividing us? Wouldn't a system willing to give up the old ideas of sexism, of viewing women as somehow inferior or different be better? They are human beings, they're equal to men in every way. In a world where men and women actually saw each other as equals, it would go a long way to creating a utopia for everyone and not just a select few in the 1 percent.

Gays: Why would anyone care what two willing adults were doing privately behind closed doors? On what basis do we use religion or personal beliefs or sexual preference to judge others? The only reason to hate and fear homosexuals or bisexuals or transsexual or anything is if it compromises our confidence in our own sexual identity, our own sexuality.

The only reason to be upset, angry or hate someone based on sexual preference is because you feel it threatens your own and that you think that if you accepted that, you may discover that you are not the specific type of straight narrow sexuality that you believed. That's part of the problem is that we've been convinced that this is so key to identity.

It's not. It isn't.

Imagine living in a world where nobody cared. Not in a negative way, but nobody got worried or got upset about who you were in a relationship with, who you were sleeping with, who you had sex with or who you were in love with.

Wouldn't that be a better world, regardless of your beliefs? Wouldn't it be a better world? Why on earth would we ever use sexuality as an excuse to treat people inhumanely, torture, kill or persecute them? There is no reason. If you have a political/religious figure that is trying to convince you of that, they are using that religion to manipulate you for their own benefit. It is for their own ends to make sure that they cause a division, so that we don't group together and stand up to them or start to question their motives. They don't want us to see the way that they are manipulating their followers. None of the religions advocate that you should go out and find a neighbour and torture, kill, maim or persecute them. Yet somehow we have so many instances where a religion or a group of people have been convinced that they should be hating someone. That's the thing. Any time that someone is using religion as an excuse for hate, they have perverted the meaning or the message of that religion.

It has been manipulated, ruined and destroyed by those that have come before. Manipulated into encouraging hatred for each other. Humanity needs to evolve beyond that emotionally and psychologically.

Like I said it doesn't affect your life. It doesn't really compromise your beliefs. If you're confident in who you are, you know who you are, and you know what your preferences are and what your sexual identity is, someone else's sexual preference and identity does not compromise yours. Its does not warrant your hatred or persecution and if we can accept that, we can come together as a human race, as humanity, and create a world where we're all free we create. A world where we're all living prosperously.

A world where we're not suffering, we're not persecuted and I feel that's the only way.

I know that that may sound hypocritical, because I said anyone trying to sway you to their way of thinking is looking out for their own interests. So I encourage you to be skeptical of what I'm saying. If you don't find that it rings true to you, then don't do it. I'm not looking to be a messiah. I'm not looking to lead. I'm not looking to profit off of this message in any way. As I mentioned before, I'll do my best to make sure that it's available free or as cheaply as possible.

I know going into this being familiar with sales channels like Kindle that you can't offer a product for less than 99 cents, so when this gets uploaded to Kindle, it'll be 99 cents, but I will do my best to look into options to offer it for free somehow. Make it available to Kindle Unlimited subscribers, to give it away. I will have contests.

I will do what I can to get this message out.

We have to stop dividing and we have to start standing up for what we feel is right and that's what I'm saying. If you don't believe what I'm saying, that's fine. Continue the way you were, but if something in what I'm saying strikes a chord, if you feel like inside of yourself that this is true, then follow that. Hang on to that. Or in your daily life, simply do what you feel is right and gravitate towards what you feel is true and truth. If you are really living your life the way that you feel is honest and true then you don't need to have any doubt. You don't need to have any second thought about what I'm saying or anyone else is saying.

Be honest with yourself. Does it feel good to you? Does it feel good to hate someone? No it doesn't. I can't say it does for me. We have to stop letting them divide us by gender, by sexual preference and by race. That's another one of the big ones.

Those in charge know that they can find petty differences and manipulate them to make us not cooperate with each other. That's the key to their success. It's that the majority don't cooperate with each other because of petty differences. When we're so busy squabbling with ourselves that we can't stop them from using us like machines.

Of course the other big divider is religion and everyone has been told and taught and brainwashed that their religion is the right way. What if they're all right? There's a huge misconception in North America that those in the Middle East worship a different being called Allah.

Not true. Do some research.

Allah is simply the Middle Eastern word for God. They're worshipping the same God as you. You've been told your entire life that they have some sort of backwards being that they worship that they believe is more true than yours, and that's not the case.

They believe in the same God as you.

So why have we been encouraged to hate them and think of them as different and backwards? Because they have a different culture? Why are we not more tolerant and understanding, that through history different cultures have developed different ways for different reasons? Why can we not honour and acknowledge and understand culture of the past, while still moving forward? Understanding that, yes you know, we developed from a more primitive way of thinking? That we came up with these ideas to explain things that didn't make sense and that we know better now, without throwing away that history? Without throwing away that past, we can respect other cultures and we can respect our own cultural past without being stuck or mired in it. We have been conditioned to fear change.

Why? Why do we abhor change?

Because we've been conditioned to feel that way, to fear change, because that's how those in charge maintain control.

If we are too afraid to rise up, because we're too apprehensive of what it's going to mean afterwards, then we're not going to rise up. We're going to be too afraid.

Dystopia now

That is part of the problem. To draw more similarities to 1984, which I understand, is a fiction novel, I think of the screens in that book. If you're not familiar with it, it's a dystopian future where everyone has a screen mounted on the wall, where the government can hear and see everything they do in their own homes and can charge them with crimes based on the things that they do and say in their own homes. Their own children are encouraged to spy on them as well, and turn mommy and daddy over if they even so much as say something that might be against the government. A government, in this case, that is trying to oppress and control and constantly monitor and surveil everyone's thoughts, opinions and ideas to weed out anything that might be subversive.

We're already living that. Are you wondering how? Well it's already been shown and proven.

Do a simple YouTube search. Here I'll even start you off with a short example: https://www.youtube.com/watch?v=ELU5g2eXi70. Government agencies have the ability to hack into your smart television, your cell phone and your other devices and use them as monitoring devices. They can access your camera and your microphone while your device isn't even turned on, or it looks like it's not turned on. Your smart TV is the same as that screen on the wall from 1984. We carry a miniature version of it with us everywhere, with our phones and when we're not on our phones, we're on our tablets and our laptops and our computers and our iPads, which all have cameras and microphones built into them.

That's how I'm creating this.

We need to come together and change the system.

THE ILLUSION OF FREEDOM

As humanity, no matter what country you live in, no matter what religion or race or sexual preference you are, we need to work together. We need to really embrace the idea of being brothers and sisters. When I say that religious leaders are perverting your opinions, that doesn't mean I'm throwing away all religious ideas or thoughts or tenants or fundamentals.

I believe they're all based on good intentions. I believe they were all created by people who saw the world the way I did or I do. Since then those who want to manipulate power for their own benefit and the detriment of others have slowly altered and changed philosophies, re-wording even, parts of religious texts.

Because they've been able to see how they could manipulate a system where their 1 percent or their Illuminati or their corporate interests could benefit.

The idea that a corporation is recognized as a person and can vote now is ridiculous. What kind of a society would have allowed that, if it wasn't already compromised? What kind of a society would allow our politics to be funded by corporate interests who create and sell products? and why would these companies need to invest this money in political campaigns?

Think about this. What are their motivations? Why would fuckin' Coca-Cola or Taco Bell or G.E. or Sony need to donate tons of money to a politician? Because they agree with their policies? I don't think so. That should be kept completely separate. If the CEO truly believes in the policies and a candidate, they should use some of their own money, those big bonuses to contribute. Only public or private citizen, I don't know how to word it properly. Only donations from private citizens from their own source of income should be allowed for funding political campaigns.

Coca-Cola is going to exist whether or not they support a political candidate. So why would they want that political candidate to owe them, unless it was to compromise them in a situation where they learn that something in that product is not good for the public, but because they've donated so much money to the political system, no one will act on it. You know why? Because these major companies and corporations, they fund both sides. They're giving money to liberals and conservatives. And guess what? That's also a false construct that's been used to divide us. They're all working for the same people, the same companies are giving them their money. So large corporations and corporate interests, they're winning no matter who wins an election, because they've provided the funding to both sides. It may not be obvious on the surface, but one company will donate money to a liberal candidate and another company would donate to a conservative candidate, and both of those companies are owned by one company above them. It's intentional and it's planned and strategic, so that shareholders and owners of these companies can maintain control. And why would they want to maintain control? Control should be in the hands of the people, our elected representatives should be representing what we want, but they're not.

Neither are some of our major religious leaders, because they're enjoying life as it is. They're enjoying, they're eating, their vacations, their paradise, but they can't see how that sort of paradise is possible without subjugating someone, without enslaving people and making them wage slaves.

Because they think; "if we don't create wage slaves, then why would they serve us?". That's another part of the problem. Instead of serving, why don't we shift our focus to helping? What if all of the places on Earth could be fed? What if the world could be an Eden? What if the world could be an Eden, simply by embracing the philosophy of helping one another? Instead of saying "Well then I'd have to get my own drink at the resort."? Maybe the person working at the bar is doing it because

THE ILLUSION OF FREEDOM

they enjoy mixing drinks for people to enjoy and maybe that server liked serving, or you know what maybe they don't, so they don't do the job, so you just walk up to the bar and get a drink instead of having to have someone deliver it to you.

I'm not saying let's put waiters out of work. There's another part of the problem too. When you hear someone presenting a solution and then someone else immediately presents a problem, that's part of conditioning. When I say what if we just went and got the drink ourselves instead of having a waitress or waiter grab it from the bar and bring it to a table, someone's going to rise up and say "Oh, but then, what are you saying?" or, you know, "I'm a waitress. Are you saying that my job isn't important or isn't needed?" No, I never said any of that, but we've been so conditioned to take offence. We've been so conditioned to respond negatively to new ideas. If you are someone who enjoys being a server or a waiter and again you're looking at it from that frame of mind, that's how you make your money to make your living. If everyone was helping each other you wouldn't need to do that, if you didn't want to, that's what I'm saying.

So what would you do if you didn't need the money? If you'd still serve, if you'd still be a waiter, then you would be able to do that and you can rely on the fact that people would show their appreciation by giving you something in return that was useful to you.

I know it's difficult.

I don't have all of the answers and the problem is, we've been conditioned to think "if we don't have all the answers then we have to disregard everything.".

That idea is simply not true.

If we're working together as an entire human race, with billions of people, with billions of minds, we will be able to come up with a solution for any gap in any plan. If we have faith in each other and work together.

We can create a utopia for everyone and stop this middle class divide. I know it sounds pie in the sky and that brings me to my next point.

It's convoluted and complicated because the system has been manipulated to be that way, and it can be overwhelming.

That's what I think has held back a lot of us as human beings. We see these things. We know what I'm saying is true, but it's such a big problem it's overwhelming. You feel defeated before you started. That's what they want. That's intentional. That keeps them in control. We need to think about possible futures and we need to think generationally. By that I mean, yes these are large problems, they're going to take a lot of work. It's going to take a lot of effort and a lot of fight to earn everyone's freedom. It may not happen in our generation, because they are such big problems, but instead of letting that overwhelm you and make you give up and not fight the system. Understand this there are possible futures if we go the direction we're going now.

Your children, grandchildren and great grandchildren are going to live in a society where they're subjugated and controlled and oppressed and they're not going to even know the difference.

They're not going to know any better and they're going to be like human machines or cattle ferried from one location to another, working to keep those in charge living comfortably. They are going to use technology to convince us that isn't the case. That we're happy and we're free and we're connecting all over, but the thing is, we're not connecting with our own humanity or people in real life.

THE ILLUSION OF FREEDOM

When the power goes out, I hope we still remember how to tell stories, how to sit around a fire and tell stories to each other and connect and communicate.

Because right now we're moving so far away from that.

Claim freedom now for your great-great grandchildren

So one possible future is that your great grandchildren never even understand or know the concept of freedom.

Or we start now.

We start today to make change, and we may not be completely free. We may be living under the illusion of freedom, in order to keep us complacent, but we can ensure that maybe our grandchildren or great grandchildren are finally part of a generation where everyone is completely free. A future where they aren't wage slaves and they're not held under the thumb or controlled by political, religious or corporate interests.

We have to do it today. We have to make changes. We have to stand up for ourselves. We have to stop accepting policies. We have to stop accepting the word of people who are trying to encourage us to hate and manipulate us. The way to a better world is to be better people and to love and cooperate with each other instead of creating walls dividing us based on differences.

There is a saying from one of my favourite movies "people shouldn't be afraid of their governments, governments should be afraid of their people."

When did you last think that was true? Can you think of any government right now in the world that is afraid of its people, more than its people are afraid of it? There are none that come to the top of my head. I could be wrong, there could be some out there, but the way this world is working, the way the system is working, doesn't feel honest and true or right to me. Anyone trying to create a division isn't doing it for good reasons.

THE ILLUSION OF FREEDOM

Think of the future think of something bigger than yourself, not just you not just your family, not just your children, not just your grandchildren or your descendants. Humanity. Do you want humanity to be free? Do you want humanity to be oppressed?

Those are the two futures we have.

We've been convinced because of economics, because of crashes, because of all of this stuff that we can't do things. We can't afford things. We've been convinced that, you know, life is too hard. In the past you could have six kids and have one person working and support a family and now you can have two people working can't afford to have one child, or can't afford to have more than one child. When you think of this, if you believe in what I'm saying, and if you can instill these beliefs even if you're not successful, if you try to instill into your own children. If you have children, instill these beliefs. You're helping create the people that are going to help free humanity in the future.

You may not be able to do it in your lifetime, but you can help inspire and encourage those thoughts, those belief systems, to survive, keep the struggle up, to create resistance so that someday we'll all truly be free. Free of the system where we owe our well-being and our ability to live and support and provide for ourselves and those we love to large, faceless corporations that are feeding us poison in one way or another. We've been conditioned to believe so many things that are untrue.

We've been conditioned to believe that you need to smoke or drink to fit in with a certain group or social class.

We've been conditioned to believe that it's almost unacceptable or anti-social to not partake in those same things, as if the fact that you have a drink in your hand somehow makes you fit in.

It's an artificial construct. Why would you care if someone else drinks or smokes just because you do. It's a personal choice, and the same goes the opposite way.

If you don't drink and don't smoke, why do you care if someone else does? Other than the fact that you care about their health and well-being. Those products that are being taxed by the government are also encouraged by the government and they are providing campaign funds that get people elected as well as keep them rich when they are in office through the taxes charged on those products, which are full of addictive poisons.

Which brings me back to the subject of marijuana.

I think it is more likely than not, that if we legalize marijuana and make it a government regulated item, under the current system, it will be perverted as well.

Same way tobacco was. We're going to find ourselves being poisoned by something that was not a poison originally, because when we get to the point where you can go buy a pack of joints just like a pack of cigarettes, there's going to be so many additives to keep us hooked and to enhance that high. There's always a chance that this whole progress being made for marijuana is the current establishment's attempt to keep people sedated and placated if we're all high and make it harder to rise up.

But I would present an alternate argument.

I don't know about some of the other drugs out there, but in the case of marijuana, the only danger it represents is making you think, and it's been portrayed in a different way.

Yes you get the munchies and yes you know there's all these funny things.

THE ILLUSION OF FREEDOM

It may affect some of your brain cells, but natural marijuana that's not been interfered with does nothing but open your mind to possibilities outside of the current system we live in. That's why it's been suppressed so much. I truly feel and believe that, and if you don't that's OK. If you think up until this point everything I've said is agreeable, except for what I'm saying of marijuana, then just take that point out of the equation and you can say "I believe in this, but I don't believe in that." and that's a personal choice and I'm not going to see you as an enemy.

We can all work together. It doesn't have to be an all or none proposition. We've been trained to think that. It doesn't have to be "oh well, you know, we all believe in these basics, but your group believes that marijuana is OK and my group doesn't. So now we have to have some sort of divide. We can't work together now and say OK, well you believe that and I believe this and we can leave those differences aside.". Something I think we forgot to do as a society, leave our differences aside and focus on how we can work together on the things we have in common what we believe in together.

I believe that everyone, every living person, every part of the population, every part of the public, every part of humanity and the billions of people on earth, we have a few basic things that we can agree on.

We don't want to suffer. We don't want to be enslaved. We don't want to be depressed. We don't want to be oppressed. We don't want to do things we would never want to do in order to make money paid by other people or corporations to support ourselves.

If we as people can support each other, then we don't have to work a horrible job. I'm not saying that there's not going to be any work, there's going to be work. Everyone has to be willing to use and develop and explore skills and talents, learn new things, learn how to be self-sufficient, learn how to grow your own food, create your own power, live off the land, cooperate with each other, share.

We may not be able to do it in our lifetime, but someday humanity can be free and living in Utopia.

If we plant the seeds now, and we may surprise ourselves, if we get enough people on board in one generation we may see the fruits of those labours. But if we don't, if we're going to have faith in anything, we have faith in all these other things; we have faith in different beliefs and deities and religions and what we need to have faith in is ourselves. We need to understand that if we work together we can create a paradise for humanity. If we don't work together, no one will ever experience that. No one will ever be free. There are so many ideas, so many things I wanted to explore in this recording, and I don't know if I will get to. Maybe I'll be fortunate that I'll be able to record another one.

To be honest I did have some fear and trepidation.

I'm still a bit worried that someday, maybe today, maybe tomorrow, a group of people are going to storm in. Take me away and I'll never be heard of again, because I'm speaking out against the current system that is in charge of the world.

I hope and I have faith that this message will reach people, and even if that fear happens, it will help to encourage humanity in the future to change things. To free themselves of the oppression that we've been deceived into accepting.

THE ILLUSION OF FREEDOM

Busy people are distracted

Think about this; why do we need packaged and processed foods? Really. Think about that.

Well they became popular because we were such busy people and so important we didn't have time to cook. Why didn't we have time to make our own food? Because we had to put in as much time as we could for the company that gives us the money to buy the goods to support our families. Isn't that convenient? You don't have to worry about cooking, you can work for me and I'll give you the money to buy the things to feed your family. But, if you weren't at that job, you could make the things to feed your family yourself. But, then where would you do it? Because you need a home, and it's not easy to do that, especially today. A lot of people aren't going to be able to afford homes.

There's a reason for that.

They don't want it like that. It's not that nobody owns the homes or the land. If the average person can't afford it, then who owns it? Who has the home and rents it to the average person? Large companies and the few, the wealthy. The one percent own where you live, and they want your money to provide your home.

So you have to go slave at a job you hate, in order to make the money just to have a place to live before you even worry about your basics like food and taking care of a family and they just want more and more. They bleed more and more from you.

Why do we need fluoride in the water? Well there wasn't enough in our systems. Why is that? Because our teeth are rotting from the fucking processed foods we're eating. They are much higher in sugar and other toxins than we would have naturally consumed.

The idea of processed and packaged foods is just another way of manipulating and perverting a world and a society in which we could live. Humans don't need processed chemicals to live. We need vitamins and minerals provided by fruits and vegetables and grains and meats that we can grow and harvest ourselves.

But instead, we've been conditioned to choose comfort. We've been conditioned to try and find ways to work less because we know that rich people don't work at all and they enjoy a life of vacations and setting their own schedules while the rest of us slave away for decades,, just in the hopes that we might be able to enjoy the last few years of our lives and possibly leave behind a positive memory or legacy with the next generation.

I think we need to aim higher.

I think we need to be working towards the absolute freedom of future generations, even if we can't enjoy that absolute freedom now.

When I say absolute freedom, I mean people can do what they want. They can live and enjoy paradise, work for themselves, provide for themselves and help each other and we're all on an equal playing field. We all have useful skills and are respected. Respecting each other for the skills that are useful and appreciating each other by providing those skills to those who help us.

Yes it sounds like an old fashioned barter system because it is. We've been deceived into believing that won't work and that we need to have paper money, cash money, imaginary credits on a plastic card in order to survive and to function as a society. We don't. Those are all functions where someone else has inserted themselves as a middleman that's not necessary, to make a profit by offering a slight convenience.

They are all things we don't need.

THE ILLUSION OF FREEDOM

When I talk about freedom. I don't mean you can do whatever you want, which I'm sure someone will make that argument, regardless of the fact that I'm clarifying it now. Some will still make that argument, but the fact is freedom when applied to everyone means that no one is unfairly abused, neglected, taken advantage of, or suffers. That may seem unrealistic and unfathomable at this time, but that's what I'm saying. It may be impossible for our generation, but if we don't act, then everyone in future generations will be oppressed, and don't get caught up in the idea that maybe you can excel and that your family will be part of that 1 percent and in a few generations they can rule and that it's not their problem because a) now you're using the suffering of humanity to benefit yourself and your progeny, and that's just wrong. You know it and you've been duped into believing that that's possible in order to keep you in line and to prevent you from cooperating with the rest of your fellow humans. Maybe if you work a little bit harder you can become the CEO and your kids are going to have every advantage in the world and they're going to be able to live life permanently on vacation. It's not going to happen. Look at the hierarchy. It's like a pyramid. If everyone on the same level as you is capable of moving up then it wouldn't work.

You all either equally have the opportunity to move up or equally are impossible to move up. Guess what? Those in the top aren't pulling you up from the lower level. In fact, they're more likely to bring in someone else from another company that was at the same level of a pyramid somewhere else to replace them, then to move someone up. That's how they maintain the power. That's how they keep that exclusive elite club at the top. They move laterally from one pyramid to another without pulling anyone up from below. They're likely going to push you back down farther if you try to hard to climb up too. It's true. You know it's true. So why not try and do something to help your fellow man and improve the lives of your future generations and work together with humanity?

What we need to do is stand up and reject this system that we've been conned into believing is the only way things work. Just like the defeatist saying "well, you know what? That's how it works, it's the best system we've got. It's not perfect, but it's all we have." No, we need to quit accepting that. We need to fix the system. We need to stop being complacent. We need to zero in on the problems and the shortcomings, on those imperfections and change them. So just saying "well that's the system we've got. We have to accept it and work with it." That isn't good enough any more. We don't have to accept it. Accepting it is a defeatist, brainwashed way of thinking.

Karmically, if you want to talk about the idea of karma, and whether you believe in karma or not, when you're doing something with good intentions to help someone else, that's when you're doing the right thing. If you're not doing that or if you're doing something negative with negative intentions to harm or manipulate someone then you're doing the wrong thing. It's really simple, but we've been manipulated with guilt. Hey listen, the establishment knows how to use guilt. Guilt is a powerful tool. So now we we have this doubt, we have the second thought where we say to ourselves "what if I do something. Good with good intentions, but then the person I do that for somehow misuses it or is misguided or things turn out negatively or they use it in a negative way? Then now I am responsible partially at the very least, for those negative things happening, even though I tried to do something good."

We need to reject that way of thinking. If you do something with nothing but good intentions to help someone and are not misguided then you are not responsible for the actions they take afterwards. They are responsible for their own actions. Case in point. You witnessed a car accident. You save someone's life and then that person kills someone. Maybe kills their wife a few years later. You are not responsible for that. You did good. You did right. You saved a life

THE ILLUSION OF FREEDOM

In the reverse, let's imagine that time travel was possible. Let's imagine we can go to the future and from the future we can travel to the past and this is a classic idea here, but if you go back in time and kill Hitler as a child and prevent World War II. Well that is not a good intention, that is causing harm and suffering to another person even if it's Hitler as a child. He hasn't become that horrible monster. Killing a child is not excusable for any reason. It would only bring negativity on you. It would be wrong, as murder is wrong and there is no excuse or positive spin you can put on it.

So will it be more acceptable to go back in time and kill Hitler as an adult at the beginning of World War II?

It's a grey area. Murder is still wrong.

I will leave you to decide that because I don't believe you can do the wrong things for the right reasons.

As much as I want to make an excuse for it, as much as I want to say killing Hitler would prevent the death of millions of innocent people. It would. Does that justify killing. I'm not sure, but I know killing a child would be wrong. I know that killing Hitler as a child, even if it's Hitler, is going to compromise you more than anything, and you would ruin your life with guilt.

In closing?

So what is the crux of my thesis here?

Well if I can bring it to a head or a point, I guess it would be that we need to work together. We need to create a generation in the future that is completely free to pursue happiness, to pursue life, to pursue love to pursue paradise and Utopia on Earth in life.

The only way we can do that is if we stop the system that we're currently stuck in. We've gone down the wrong road. We've allowed ourselves to be misled by people who want to manipulate and control. We've allowed ourselves to be oppressed and become slaves to corporations, slaves to religious leaders and slaves to political figures, in order to maintain their comfort on our suffering.

Whether you are black, white, yellow, brown, red, anything, we need to work together. Accept our fellow man for each other's mutual freedom, whether you're Christian, Muslim, Hindu, Buddhist, or anything else. We can accept each other's beliefs and work together for everyone's mutual freedom.

Our system and society, our politic,s religion, our beliefs, our very identities have been compromised by people who need us to be slaves, to earn imaginary money to scrape by and help build their stock of imaginary money in order so that they never have to be slaves like the ones that they control.

As I said I worried about the response from the system to these words. If this material is censored, any government, organization or sales channel that censors this material is giving it credibility and credence.

And if they don't censor it, it gets out.

So it's a win-win.

By not censoring it, I can share this idea. By censoring, you're showing this idea has merit and has at least some truth to it. So I'm in a no-lose situation, which is exactly what I want. I worry about being targeted, but I may release this under a different name. I may work through like-minded people. I may keep my true identity concealed, though I feel I shouldn't have to. I feel I'm speaking the truth and that in speaking the truth that I need to set an example for everyone to not be afraid to say these things out loud to not be afraid to talk about them, to not be afraid to believe in them, to not be afraid, to encourage others to take back their freedom. That's all we need to do.

We need to take back our freedom.

I hope you can do that. I hope you can be a part of that, but if not, know that I understand and that I love and care about you and your freedom. No matter who you are, no matter where you live. I truly believe someday we will be able to be truly free and I hope that you and your children are there to see it, even if you never believe what I'm saying. Even if you believe that this book is the ramblings of a madman.

We need to be free. Humanity needs to be free.

Thank you.

Addendum: Aliens, Time Travel, Conspiracy, Religion, Slavery – The System

In this recording, or book, I've tried to present as much as I can of my stream of thought and consciousness and ideas, but I know I'll never fit it all. Not right now. Maybe I'll make some follow up recordings, but here are a few subjects that I wanted to cover really quickly.

One: Aliens; do they exist? I don't know. I think it's a possibility. It also might not be, but if they do exist, they may be involved with those that have created a system that oppresses us, but that could be just fantasy. Or it could be reality, and if it is reality, it is a reality that we can overcome. As humans we have to keep in mind that it's working together that will help us overcome any challenge regardless of how big or how crazy it may sound.

I know I'm getting into some weird territory, I just want to remind everybody that I am no longer high and so these are no longer the ramblings of someone who is stoned and that I still believe the things I'm saying to be true. They feel right and honest to me and that's what I have to go with.

Two: Time travel; Is it possible? I don't know. We may discover it in the future. I feel like we must discover it in the future and that maybe there are those in the future who have misused the technology, gone back in time and created this kind of system that we're living under and perverted freedom and humanity for people so that they and their descendants will benefit. I feel like that's the only way that it could have been proven to those in charge that this agenda would have worked. Again I could be totally wrong, and if I am that's fine, because whether I am wrong or not, whether I'm wrong or right, the issue still exists that we as a human race are enslaved by those who force us to work to buy things we don't need. There needs to be a change in the system. Nobody is going to be 100 percent right. I'm not trying to present myself as some sort of messiah or leader. I'm just presenting my feelings and my thoughts.

I don't think we need a new leader, I think we need a new unity among the human race. That will lead us to choosing better new leaders.

What about people who just represent everything you're diametrically opposed to?

Well, you'll meet them. I know some and I believe those people are sent to challenge you, but just because you meet someone who you feel morally and ethically completely opposed to, doesn't mean you should lose faith in humanity.

These people are there to make you lose faith in other people.

I believe honestly and strongly and wholeheartedly that the majority of people can come to realize the truth of what I'm saying. That we need to come together and that those that enjoy profiting off the sorrow of others or using, manipulating or leeching off their fellow man without contributing, they've just been compromised so much by the system that they've begun to embody it. Those people may save themselves. They may change their ways when a new example is given or they may not and if they don't that's fine. That's not a reflection on you and it shouldn't reflect your beliefs and feelings on other people. Let that negative person inherit their own karma and let them struggle to meet a new system. Those who thrive on negativity will be weeded out or change their ways when they're in a system where they have to cooperate and share with their neighbour.

Conspiracy; there's a lot of definitions or feelings or things associated with that word, "conspiracy". What I'm describing is definitely a conspiracy. Those that conspire to maintain control and power over society, over the world and oppress the majority. So yes, I believe in conspiracy. Do I believe in every conspiracy? Probably not, but I do believe conspiracy exists and that it is purposely given a negative connotation in order to make people not stand up and make change and speak out. That's the biggest thing that we need right now. People brave enough to stand up and speak out and say that the system doesn't work.

It's perverted and it needs to be fixed.

I hope that you will all join me in this belief. I hope we will bring a new future to humanity as quickly as possible, because we need it.

We are on the verge of potential catastrophe.

'm not trying to be one of those people that profit from these doomsday predictions. I've never been one of those people. I've always dismissed them. I've always been optimistic for the future, but the last year or two, let's be honest, the last decade, things have rapidly progressed in a negative way.

I've lost faith in our political systems, our politicians and it's time that humanity took their freedom back.

I hope that we can all work together as brothers and sisters in humanity, and I look forward to working with you all.

I keep thinking I'm done with this recording and then realizing that I'm subconsciously holding back because I'm afraid to say things and beliefs that might show a bias toward any particular religion or train of thought that could be divisive. I'll say this; I am not part of, affiliated or identify with any organized religion, but I believe there is a reason that some of the tenets that we find in various religions exist. If we lived in a world where we all helped each other and respected each other and were free to do what we wanted, so far as it didn't harm or hurt or force anybody to do anything against their will, we would all be happier. When we look at things like the seven deadly sins, I can agree with those things. For the majority of them anyway.

Or the Ten Commandments. You shouldn't kill or murder because it causes suffering to another human being whose life has equal value to yours, regardless of their social or economic status.

We shouldn't steal from someone because stealing causes unnecessary stress and emotional trauma. As badly as you think you may need something, the person you're stealing from may need it more. Under dire circumstances when a person or a family is starving, stealing a loaf of bread is excusable, but under the system that I propose, where we all help each other, stealing food wouldn't be necessary. Stealing personal belongings, again, in a world where everyone's helping each other, there would be no need to steal, because everyone would have their own skills and abilities that they could offer in exchange. So you could approach a baker and offer to fix a window, clean their eavestrough, to build something and they would show their appreciation by offering you some of their goods.

Thou shall not covet thy neighbour's wife: That's a big one and that's one that we've really moved away from and really forgotten about. This is why you shouldn't: If you have to lust after someone else's wife, you're only causing a situation of unhappiness and misery for yourself and them. Either they aren't going to reciprocate and you are always going to feel unhappy and unfulfilled, lusting after something you can't have. We've all been brainwashed to believe that this is natural and is part of the human experience. With positive thinking and positive mindset, letting go of old insecurities, the situation shouldn't arise. You would be confident that you can find someone just beautiful, just as wonderful as the person you are lusting after.

If your feelings are reciprocated then you're causing emotional trauma and distress to existing family and ruining an existing relationship or an existing marriage.

There is one minor exception.

If a man wants to share his wife, and his wife wants to be shared and take part in the activity and everyone is a consenting and willing adult and no one is being coerced and forced, then there's nothing wrong with that. We shouldn't impose our beliefs or feelings on someone else or use it to divide us and cause to fight with each other.

Again what happens between willing adults behind closed doors is no one else's business.

Now what if a man wants to share the wife and his wife doesn't want to be shared? There rises another issue: Someone feeling unfulfilled in their desires and fantasies. If that person can't overcome that desire, then those two people shouldn't be together. They should be happy and willing to find a partner that has the same feelings and beliefs and desires and fantasies as them. There's a lot of people out there. Instead of being mired in unhappiness and obligated to stay together when you don't have similar interests and you don't want to participate in each other's desires.

Going back to the subject of food. I actually had said some of the stuff already, bu the recording had stopped without me noticing, so I'm trying to recreate what I was saying earlier in my stream of thought.

Getting to the point; we need to stop buying and eating the food that poisons us and supporting the companies that make it. We need to realize that if something comes in a box or a plastic package that's sealed or glued in a factory, that we shouldn't eat it. We don't need all these processed and packaged foods. They do nothing, but make us addicted. We are clearly addicted. The fact that the majority of the population doesn't want to even consider or admit that is a sign that they're addictive.

The fact that we can't even examine it. We are addicted to the sugars and the additives and artificial compounds that are found in food that shouldn't be allowed. If we all quit buying these food products tomorrow,

THE ILLUSION OF FREEDOM

these companies wouldn't be able to sustain themselves, because they have built themselves on a model that we're never going to stop buying because we're so addicted. If we made that choice tomorrow, these companies wouldn't have the money they needed to fund political campaigns and thereby distort and pervert public interest by buying politicians. That's really what it comes down to. If we stopped buying these things, these products, the things we consume that we're addicted to: food, cigarettes, alcohol. I'm not saying "don't buy food", I'm saying: don't buy processed food. Fruits, vegetables, meats, breads and grains, those are all you need and they are easy to come by in a lot of places. It doesn't take that much effort to learn how to produce them yourself,. if you need to. We need to stop supporting these companies that are poisoning us and distorting our morals, our ethics and our society. Our system.

Our System.

We need to stand up and make that choice, and a lot of us, our willpower has been ruined. That's how they want it. That's been orchestrated too. They want us to be addicted. You can say "oh I know I shouldn't eat this, but it tastes just so good" and you feel like it's not a big deal. Just a few extra calories a day, but the stakes are much bigger than that. When you give in to that impulse to poison yourself with something that taste delicious, but you know is bad for you, you're not just selling a few calories in your day for that taste of well-being. You're selling the future, you're selling the hopes and the very freedom of humanity, of your descendants for your momentary pleasure, for your enjoyment of that cigarette or that Hostess cupcake, you're trading the freedom of future generations for your momentary pleasure. Freedom is the most important thing we should all protect and all work together to do our part to ensure that it continues to exist in the future and that future generations are freer than we are now.

It's really the only option. If you value life and freedom and if you want there to be any chance to escape wage slavery in your lifetime we have to act now. You may feel yourselves in immense pressure, in situations already working for these companies and not able to leave for financial reasons or obligations or not wanting to be judged.

That's all part of their plan. They need to keep you under their thumb; so I'll say this: We can use their systems against them, just like using technology and Internet to deliver this message and use their own sales channels against them because they are built on greed and if something sells they will sell it, even if it undermines their own system. If they go as far as to censor it, it's the same as admitting that what I'm saying is true. It's a win-win for me. It's a lose-lose for them, because they are so greedy they will trade the money they'll make off my message for that momentary gain. They will risk that the message will completely undermine them because they are governed by greed.

So if they think they can make a dollar off of my message, they will, but ultimately that message will continue to spread until they can't make a dollar on anything and no longer can influence public policy and religious and political leaders. They do that. They don't just buy politicians. Don't fool yourself.

There are a lot of business and corporate interests funding various religious figures too. Back to the idea of people stuck working for these companies and using their systems to undermine them, we can take them down from the inside.

You can do your part by weakening their systems from the inside and it's not espionage and it's not underhanded and it's not deceitful.

Why? Because they already infiltrated us. They infiltrated humanity and they divided us and they conquered us and they took over and they have enslaved us ever since. It is only fair and just that we reverse that. We need to infiltrate them and take them down.

Support your local businesses, your local farmer, your local craftspeople. Barter and trade with them. Go to an independent family owned restaurant instead of a chain. Make food at home instead of buying fast food.

If we all work together and help each other this system that oppresses us wouldn't be necessary. We need to make drastic change. The only way we're going to do it is if we take down these monsters. Think of the biblical story of David and Goliath. Again I'm not pushing any religion here, but the symbolism is what's important. We may be small, but together we can be mighty. We can take down those giant corporations that are poisoning us and deceiving us.

The only way we do that is if we band together and we need to. We need to set aside our petty differences. We need to focus on what we believe in common that people should be treated with respect. Anyone trying to create a division, whether it's a business person or politician or religious leader, if they're trying to encourage you to segregate from someone else or another group based on petty differences; belief, gender, sexual preference, they are infiltrating and undermining the unity of the human race. They are causing divisions so that we're easier to conquer, so that we can't work together because we've been convinced that these minor differences somehow are major offences. They're not. A major offence is trying to encourage hatred between your fellow man. Addiction. Poisoning people for profit. Those are the real egregious violations of humanity. Those are the things we need to stop. We don't need to worry about our neighbour and whether they like men or women. it doesn't matter. The men or women that they like can be part of our system to help overthrow the oppressive regime that has taken over humanity and is controlling our world.

We're living in the illusion that there are governments and countries. It's all owned by corporations now. It really is. We already live in a one world government, we just don't know it. We're given the illusion of borders and nations and are given the illusion of freedom, so that will stay in line. We need a revolution and we need to start today. We need to take a risk. We need to risk looking foolish to others.

It's the only way we're going to break free from a cycle that pushes poverty onto its people and suffering. That's what all of these movements over time have been about. That's why Anonymous exists. That's why the Occupy movement happened.

All leading up to this. We need to band together for humanity.

We need to say "No more!". We need to make a change. We need to do it today. I wholeheartedly hope that's what I have done.

That's what I have: Hope. I have hope for the future still, in spite of everything that I've described, that's gone wrong, that's been distorted and perverted and manipulated and things that have gone horribly bad, they were necessary for us to realize that we can not stand for them.

Join me. Join me today and let's make a better future where everyone is free.

Don't miss out!

Visit the website below and you can sign up to receive emails whenever Mike Gagnon publishes a new book. There's no charge and no obligation.

https://books2read.com/r/B-A-RBQB-BYSP

BOOKS 2 READ

Connecting independent readers to independent writers.

Also by Mike Gagnon

Orlok
Orlok

Standalone
Skidsville
The Island of Dr. Morose
The Illusion of Freedom
A Letter to the Middle East
A Western Gentleman
Project Magenta

Watch for more at www.mikegagnon.ca.

About the Author

Mike Gagnon is an author living in the Niagara Region of Canada.

He has been a professional writer and comic creator since 2000. He has written, illustrated and edited hundreds of books, articles and graphic novels.

Mike has worked for publishers of all sizes, from Marvel Comics to many small press publishers.

For more info visit: www.mikegagnon.ca

Read more at www.mikegagnon.ca.